The Skinny on Bullying

the skinny on™
bullying

the legend of
gretchen

Mike Cassidy

ISBN: 978-0-9824390-1-2
Ebook ISBN: 978-0-9844418-4-6
Library of Congress: 2010938897

Illustration / Design: Lindy Nass   Kim Lincon

For information address Rand Media Co, 265 Post Road West, Westport, CT, 06880 or call (203) 226-8727.

The Skinny On™ books are available for special promotions and premiums. For details contact: Donna Hardy, call (203) 222-6295 or visit our website: www.theskinnyon.com

Printed in the United States of America
The Country Press, INC.

9 2 5 – 4 9 1 9
10 9 8 7 6 5 4 3 2

INTRODUCTION

MESSAGE TO THE BULLIED:

Let's face it… bullying exists.

There are so many forms of bullying that it's IMPOSSIBLE to give a one size fits all solution to the problem. Every instance of bullying is unique. Bullying happens in every country and culture in the world. Everyone, including parents and adults, has experienced some type of bullying in their lifetime.

Some of the strategies in this book may be helpful to you while others may not. Always use your common sense and judgment when dealing with a bully and make personal safety your #1 priority. Remember this book is a guide, not the answer to bullying. If you have a problem with bullying, I recommend you exercise this book's *Golden Rule:* talk to an adult. Together you can devise a strategy that is best for your particular situation.

MESSAGE TO THE BULLIES:

If you are reading this book you are taking the first steps towards improving your behavior. Not only is bullying uncool, there are also serious consequences for kids who bully. You can be suspended from school, expelled, or even arrested. A good exercise is to put yourself in the shoes of the kid you are bullying. How would you feel in their position? Remember, if you don't want it done to you, DON'T DO IT TO OTHERS! Always remember this book's *Golden Rule:* talk to an adult. If you are serious about putting an end to bullying, talk to an adult you trust. Don't worry about getting into trouble. You're doing the right thing!

"In the end it is not the words of our enemies we will remember, but the silence of our friends."

Martin Luther King, Jr.

Hi, I'm Mike Cassidy. Growing up I was bullied. I was also (at times) a bit of a bully myself. Based on my experiences, I think it's fair to say I understand what it's like on both sides of the problem.

I've also spoken with experts including parents, teachers, coaches, psychologists, and counselors to give you the best advice around.

As you are reading, keep an eye out for words that are **BOLD, CAPITALIZED, AND UNDERLINED**. These words will be defined in the glossary at the end of the book.

I'D LIKE TO INTRODUCE YOU TO BILLY AND BETH. THEY ARE 10 YEARS OLD.

THEY ARE NEIGHBORS.

1

THEY'VE BEEN BEST FRIENDS FOR AS LONG AS THEY CAN REMEMBER.

2

THEY DO EVERYTHING TOGETHER.

EVERYONE PRETTY MUCH THINKS THEY ARE BOYFRIEND AND GIRLFRIEND ... BUT THEY MOST DEFINITELY ARE _NOT_.

"No way."

"Ick!"

LAST YEAR, BILLY AND BETH GRADUATED 5TH GRADE. THEY WERE PRETTY POPULAR AT STICKVILLE ELEMENTARY SCHOOL.

STICKVILLE ELEMENTARY SCHOOL

5

BILLY WAS THE CLASS PRESIDENT.

"If I'm voted president, I pledge to get our class a brand new snack machine!"

6

BUT ALL THAT CHANGED THE DAY THEY SHIPPED OFF TO STICKVILLE MIDDLE SCHOOL TO START 6TH GRADE.

NOW, A NEW SCHOOL AWAITS THEM...

A MYSTERIOUS LAND UNKNOWN TO ALL ON BOARD...

THE MIDDLE SCHOOL'S NATIVES ARE BIG AND STRONG AND THEY DON'T LOOK LIKE THEY TAKE KINDLY TO STRANGERS.

BUT THE BRAVE SAILORS FEARLESSLY SAIL FORWARD ON A NEW ADVENTURE.

WHAT WILL THIS NEW WORLD HOLD FOR THEM? *ONLY TIME WILL TELL...*

UPON ARRIVAL, BILLY AND BETH REALIZE THAT THEY AREN'T GOING TO BE AS POPULAR AS THEY USED TO BE.

CHANGING SCHOOLS CAN BE A DIFFICULT TRANSITION

A new school means new freedoms, people, classes, and responsibilities.

The best thing you can do is prepare and organize yourself for your first day. Don't let yourself get too nervous. Discuss any concerns you have with an adult you trust. Enjoy yourself. Being in school should be fun!

IN THEIR FIRST MONTH AT STICKVILLE MIDDLE SCHOOL, BILLY AND BETH HAVE BEEN <u>BY-STANDERS</u> TO BULLYING BY THE BIGGER 8TH GRADERS.

"CAN WE TALK ABOUT THIS!?!"

15

WHAT IS <u>BULLYING?</u>

A lot of young people have a good idea of what bullying is because they see it every day! Bullying happens when someone hurts or scares another person on purpose and the person being bullied has a hard time defending himself or herself. Usually, bullying happens over and over. Bullying also can happen online or electronically. Cyberbullying is when children or teens bully each other using the Internet, mobile phones, or other cyber technology.

Stop Bullying Now, HHS.gov

16

A **BULLYING POLICY** can vary from school to school. It's best to talk to a parent or teacher to learn exactly how bullying is defined at your school.

THERE ARE FOUR MAIN TYPES OF BULLYING

1. **PHYSICAL** - Intentionally hurting someone with force

2. **VERBAL** - Using words to hurt others

3. **INDIRECT** - When you hurt someone behind their back, not to their face

4. **CYBERBULLYING** - Bullying that occurs online or electronically

BILLY AND BETH HAVE BEEN LUCKY SO FAR. THEY'VE MANAGED TO STAY UNDER THE BULLYS' RADAR.

LESTER PICKLES HAS NOT BEEN AS FORTUNATE. HE'S A COMMON <u>TARGET</u> FOR BULLIES LIKE CHRIS LOGAN AND HIS <u>HENCHMEN</u>. BY THE LOOK OF IT, HE'S HAVING A HARD TIME AT SCHOOL.

"Beth! Do you see the size of that kid!?! He could smash me into jelly. I think it's better if I just keep my mouth shut."

"Billy, you should say something."

Billy and Beth, I'm going to call a time out. I've noticed you've stayed under the bullies' radar so far and that's great. Unfortunately, avoiding bullies simply is NOT ENOUGH. You need to STAND UP to bullying whenever you see it, ESPECIALLY when it involves someone else.

HOW CAN YOU HELP A VICTIM OF BULLYING?

1. *The Golden Rule:* Talk to an adult
2. **STAND UP TO THE BULLY**
3. **BE AN <u>ALLY</u>:** Lend a helping hand

1. *The Golden Rule:*

If you don't feel safe confronting the bully yourself, **talk to an adult**. You can talk to a teacher, principal, parent, counselor, nurse, coach, or any adult you trust. Make sure you tell them exactly what happened. (If they don't do anything to help, tell someone else!)

2. Stand up to the bully: If you feel safe, tell the bully to stop. It's important to establish that bullying is *not cool at your school*.

3. Be an ally: Lend a helping hand to those being bullied. You can listen to their problems, walk them home from school, invite them to join your friends, or tell them you understand what they are going through. These small things can make a BIG difference in someone's life.

"You know, Lester, we are going to audition for the 6th grade play, *The Wizard of Oz*. You should come try out with us."

"Ehh... I don't know. I'm not a very good actor. What if I get stage fright and forget my lines?"

"Don't worry, Lester. We're gonna practice everyday after school. And some of the parts only have a few words."

MR. GRISWALD'S SCIENCE CLASS, THE NEXT DAY.

"Good morning class, settle down. Today, I have prepared a special presentation using the rules of the ocean to demonstrate how you kids can avoid bullies. As you know, the ocean is filled with creatures big and small. The smaller creatures stand little chance against a big, hungry shark. In order to stay alive, the smaller animals have learned certain tricks to avoid being eaten for dinner."

Science Class

31

HOW TO AVOID BEING BULLIED

32

I.

STAY IN GROUPS

Some fish travel in a "school" just like you kids. The main reason is that there is power in numbers. Fish gain specific advantages by traveling together in groups.

A. By staying active in a group, fish have more eyes to look out for sharks. The sooner one of the fish spots the predator, the more quickly the group can flee.

"Shark!"

"Look out!"

"Let's get outta here!!!"

B. Another benefit of "schooling" is that large groups are less likely to be attacked by a predator because the group looks like a bigger, scarier animal.

C. Finally, it's harder for predators to pick out individual prey in a group because many moving fish confuse and distract the predator. When a fish is alone, it becomes an easy target.

LESSON LEARNED:

Stay active: Like the fish in our lesson, students are better off staying together with friends in a group. Stay active and participate in as many groups and clubs as you can. The more involved you are in school, the more people will be around you. It's harder for a bully to pick out a single target in a group.

II.
AVOID HOT SPOTS

"Once a shark sets his eyes on a small seal, it has little chance to escape. Sharks tend to gather in areas like shallow water and feeding grounds where seals are an easy target. These areas are called **HOT** **SPOTS**."

In order to avoid being eaten, seals have developed strategies to avoid hot spots. Some seals have learned to hunt in deep water where sharks do not look for them.

LESSON LEARNED:

Avoid hot spots: Do your best to avoid unsupervised areas where bullies might hang out.

III.
STAY CONFIDENT

Puffer fish are very slow and have poor reflexes, making them an easy target for predators. In order to stay alive, puffer fish have developed a unique ability to fill their stomachs with water so they appear to be much larger than they actually are. This scares the predator and gives the puffer a few extra seconds to escape.

43

LESSON LEARNED:

Stay confident: A bully tends to target people who seem to lack confidence or have a low self-esteem. Always try to project confidence and inner strength. Believe in yourself, take pride in your accomplishments, exercise, and eat healthy. If you follow these steps, you might be able to scare the bully off.

44

WRAP-UP

1. **Stay In Groups**: Stay active, participate, socialize, and get involved

2. **Avoid Hot Spots**: Do your best to avoid where bullying occurs

3. **Stay Confident**: Believe in yourself, take pride in your accomplishments, exercise, and be healthy

ONE WEEK LATER ...

TODAY, ALL THE STUDENTS WHO TRIED OUT FOR THE 6TH GRADE PLAY ARE CHECKING THE BULLETIN BOARD TO SEE IF THEY GOT A PART.

"Wow! I'm playing the part of Dorothy."

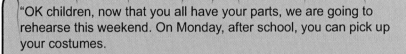

"OK children, now that you all have your parts, we are going to rehearse this weekend. On Monday, after school, you can pick up your costumes.

Also, I just learned that Suzy Ruby, who was going to play the Wicked Witch is sick at home with Chicken Pox, so the part of the witch is still available. It is a very important role, so please see if any of your friends are interested."

THE NEXT DAY, IN THE LUNCHROOM.

57

58

BILLY'S HOUSE, LATER THAT NIGHT.

"Ronnie, are you finally going to tell us your super important story?"

"Yes, and you all need to hear this. But I have to be honest, you're not going to like it."

"If any of you have a weak stomach, I suggest you go into the house for some snacks. This story is not for the faint of heart."

"Ronnie, you're being ridiculous!"

"Just tell us, Ronnie!"

"OK, you asked for it …

OUR STORY BEGINS ON A DARK, STORMY NIGHT IN THE MOUNTAINS OF TRANSYLVANIA …"

65

"Atop the highest mountain was a castle surrounded by darkness. It was one of the worst storms in years.

Over the noise of the storm, the distant sound of howling could be heard.

Owooooooooo…. OWOOOOOOOO!!!"

"Stop it, Ronnie!!! You're scaring me!"

66

"On this haunted evening, a baby was born. The child was not human. It was a daughter from nature's two greatest monsters ...

The Vampire and Werewolf ..."

"The child was pure evil and answered to only one haunted name ...

GRETCHEN!!!"

"Gretchen was born with razor-like horns, fangs, and claws. At birth, she was taken from her parents and raised by a pack of wolves. For years, the wolves scoured the country, searching for prey. At age three, Gretchen was the pack's greatest hunter…"

"One day the wolves realized Gretchen was growing too powerful. So they sent her back to live with the humans.

Legend has it that she was never able to fit in with people and, in time, her hunger returned. Gretchen found one type of target that made a particularly easy and delicious meal ... KIDS!!! Just like us. "

"OK Ronnie, that's enough. You're scaring us."

"Wait! This is the important part. It was my cousin Chip who first told me this terrible tale. Gretchen arrived at his school a few months ago and she terrorized everyone in sight."

"Oh Ronnie, you're so silly. Do you ever listen to yourself? You're talking about ancient castles and werewolf vampire babies. This is ridiculous."

"It's all real, every word. I promise."

"Even if there was a real monster out there, she is not here in Stickville. We're all safe, no kids have gone missing. There's nothing to worry about."

"I wasn't finished!!! So the other day Chip called me. He said the monster left his school to move to another unfortunate town. What town you ask... *STICKVILLE!!! NEXT MONDAY!!!*"

"That's terrible!"

"What are we going to do?"

73

"Listen, just stick with me girls, I'll protect you. The Ron Ron fears no one!"

74

CLASS, MONDAY MORNING

WIZARD OF OZ
AFTER-SCHOOL REHEARSAL.

85

"Hey Mom, look at those nerds. Hahahaha! Look at their ridiculous costumes! HAHAHAHA!!!"

"Gretchen, this is your first day sweetheart, try to be nice.

86

93

94

GRETCHEN STARTED SCHOOL THE NEXT DAY AND HER WAVE OF DESTRUCTION BEGAN.

LET'S TAKE A LOOK BACK AT THE FOUR TYPES OF BULLYING.

1. **VERBAL**

2. **PHYSICAL**

3. **INDIRECT**

4. **CYBERBULLYING**

---

1. VERBAL BULLYING

Billy and Beth just experienced **VERBAL BULLYING**. Examples include:

- Teasing
- Mocking
- Name calling
- Pranking
- Taunting

- Ridiculing
- Swearing
- Blackmailing
- Threatening

VERBAL BULLYING: WHAT TO DO?

- *The Golden Rule:* Talk to an adult

- Do not insult the bully back

- Turn and walk away from the bully, just ignore them!

2. PHYSICAL BULLYING

PHYSICAL BULLYING is aggressive behavior that causes any form of physical pain or discomfort. This can include pushing, shoving, slapping, punching, spitting, and confinement. It can also include vandalism and defacing others' stuff.

BILLY EXPERIENCED GRETCHEN'S PHYSICAL BULLYING FOR WEEKS.

101

GRETCHEN WAS A REAL PRO. SHE REALLY LET BILLY HAVE IT.

102

AND THAT'S NOT ALL...

Shoe-Lacings

Spitballs

Wedgies

Thumbtacks

Wet Willies

PHYSICAL BULLYING: WHAT TO DO?

- *The Golden Rule:* Talk to an adult

- Avoid violence at all cost

- Don't hit back

- Avoid hot spots

- Walk or run away from the bully before trouble starts

Beth, on the other hand, doesn't realize that Gretchen is bullying her. This is because Beth is being indirectly bullied.

INDIRECT BULLYING is bullying that is done behind someone's back. This doesn't mean it's harmless. In fact, it can be WORSE than physical bullying.

3. INDIRECT BULLYING

- Spreading vicious and nasty rumors
- Giving dirty looks and gestures
- Public humiliation
- Excluding or ignoring

GRETCHEN HAS BEEN SPREADING RUMORS ABOUT BETH AT SCHOOL. NOW GIRLS ARE GIVING HER WEIRD LOOKS IN THE HALLWAYS ...

107

SOMEONE KEEPS PUTTING GARBAGE ON HER BUS SEAT ...

108

AND NONE OF THE GIRLS WANT TO SIT WITH HER IN THE LUNCHROOM.

IT'S A GOOD THING FRIENDS ARE ALWAYS THERE WHEN YOU NEED THEM.

INDIRECT BULLYING: WHAT TO DO?

- *The Golden Rule:*
  Talk to an adult

- Pick good friends who treat you with respect

- Avoid getting emotional and reacting to the rumor, that's just what the bully wants

- Don't get involved in the spreading of rumors

- Talk to friends you know and trust, they will stand by you

- Remember all rumors pass with time

4. <u>CYBERBULLYING</u>

BETH'S HOUSE, LATER THAT EVENING.

BETH GETS A TEXT MESSAGE FROM BILLY...

Stick Cellular —

From: Billy

we hav 2 do something! did u c the stuff gretchen's been facebooking?

OPTIONS | OK | REPLY

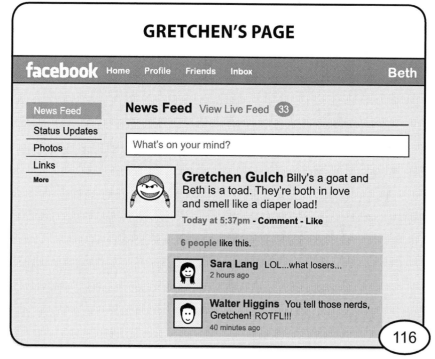

BETH GOES ON TO READ MORE TAUNTS, INSULTS, AND RUMORS...

"Oh no! Everyone in school can see this, my life is ruined! No wonder everyone's been staring, pointing and laughing at me.

I should say something mean back."

BUT INSTEAD OF RESPONDING ANGRILY, BETH GOES SEARCHING TO LEARN MORE...

Google

What is cyberbullying?|

Advanced Search
Language Tools

Google Search   I'm Feeling Lucky

Advertising Programs - Business Solutions - About Google

©2010 - Privacy

119

WHAT IS CYBERBULLYING:

Bullying can happen online or electronically. **CYBERBULLYING** is when children or teens bully each other using the Internet, mobile phones, or other cyber technology.

This can include:

- Sending mean text, email, or instant messages
- Posting nasty pictures or messages about others
- Using someone else's user name to spread rumors or lies about someone

The U.S. Department of Health and Human Services (HHS)

120

CYBERBULLYING FACTS:

- Over 40% of all teenagers with internet access have reported being bullied online.

- Only 10% of kids who are cyberbullied tell their parents about the incident.

- Experts believe that social networking sites will soon be the primary source of cyberbullying.

- Girls are more likely than boys to be the target of cyberbullying.

The National Crime Prevention Center

WHERE DOES CYBERBULLYING OCCUR?

- Chat rooms
- Email
- Websites
- Blogs
- Live video game chat
- Cell phones (texts messages)
- Instant Messenger
- Social networking sites (Facebook, Myspace, Twitter)

TYPES OF CYBERBULLYING:

- Using websites to post hurtful information
- Stealing someone's password to post damaging information
- **POSING** (building fake profiles)
- Sending computer viruses
- Altering photos in order to hurt someone
- Recording conversations without someone's consent and posting it online.
- Creating mean polls about kids
- **FLAMING** (online fights between individuals)

The National Crime Prevention Center

123

BETH CONTINUES HER RESEARCH...

124

Google

cyberbullying tips and advice|

Advanced Search
Language Tools

Google Search   I'm Feeling Lucky

Advertising Programs - Business Solutions - About Google

©2010 - Privacy

125

CYBERBULLYING TIPS AND ADVICE

- *The Golden Rule:*
  Talk to an adult

- Don't respond (like Beth almost did)

- Use block features where you can so the bully can't contact you

- Don't post anything on the internet you don't want to be there forever

- Use privacy features so bullies can't find you

- Don't send messages when you are angry

- Think twice about everything you send

- Always be mindful of who is taking your photograph

- Don't erase messages (SAVE EVERYTHING COLLECT EVIDENCE)

- Don't participate in social networks (it's not mandatory)

126

LET BULLIES KNOW THE CONSEQUENCES OF CYBERBULLYING:

- Bullies can be suspended or expelled from school

- Bullies can lose their Instant Messenger, Facebook, and other accounts permanently

- Bullies can have the internet access to their house terminated

- Bullies can be charged with a crime

Whoa, here's a list of famous people who were bullied when they were kids.

Eminem (Grammy and Academy Award Winner)

"I would change schools two, three times a year and that was probably the roughest part.

"[I got] beat up in the bathroom, beat up in the hallways, shoved in the lockers, just, for the most part, being the new kid."
(*60 Minutes Interview*, October 10, 2010)

Taylor Swift (Grammy Award Winning Singer)

Before she was famous, Taylor Swift used to get picked on in high school.
"Growing up on a Christmas tree farm was basically a shunning – and that's never a good thing, you know ... A lot of girls thought I was weird. Actually, the word they liked to use was "annoying" ... I'd sit at their lunch table and they'd move to a different one."
(Swift, 18, in *Women's Health Magazine,* December 2008)

Taylor Lautner (the star of *Twilight*)

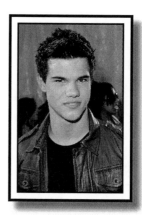

"I was never extremely confident ... Because I was an actor, when I was in school there was a little bullying going on. Not physical bullying but people making fun of what I do ... I just had to tell myself I can't let this get to me. This is what I love to do. And I'm going to continue to do it." (*Interview with Rolling Stone Magazine,* December 10, 2009)

Kate Winslet (Academy Award Winner)

The actress Kate Winslet was tormented at school because of her weight. *"I became shy because I was overweight ... at 16 I was called "Blubber". It was pathetic and childish, but girls are so catty. It lasted for about two years. Eventually, I must have told my mother, and she took it up with the teachers."* (*The UK Observer,* November 4, 2001)

BETH DECIDES IT'S FINALLY TIME TO TALK TO AN ADULT. SHE WANTS TO TELL HER PARENTS BUT SHE THINKS THEY MAY OVERREACT.

This celebrity stuff is really cool. I'm going to send this to Billy. I think I'll talk to a grown up about our problem tomorrow.

133

BETH REMEMBERED

The Golden Rule:

Talk to an adult!

134

The Golden Rule:

The first thing you should always do if you are being bullied is talk to an adult, even if you have a hard time talking to someone older.

Talk to an adult you know and trust, and tell them everything that is happening to you. Tell them how you are feeling and ask them how they will help keep you safe.

It's the responsibility of parents and teachers to make sure you're being treated fairly. Don't be afraid that the bully will find out. You are better off with the situation out in the open.

Bullies thrive on secrecy.

WRAP-UP

Regardless of the type of bullying you're experiencing, dealing with a bully can be a terrible experience. New technology makes it easier than ever to hurt others. You might feel like there's no hope. You might feel alone. But you should know that there are thousands of kids all over the world who are just like you. No matter how sad bullying makes you feel, don't ever think there's nothing you can do to stop it. Don't ever think that bullying is your fault. Hurting others is never acceptable behavior. EVER.

141

142

Beth followed *The Golden Rule*

She talked to an adult and now actions are being taken to put an end to the bullying.

Sometimes an adult might not do everything they should to help. If you feel you still need help, talk to another adult until you feel safe.

BETH'S AFTERNOON SOCCER PRACTICE

"Alright everyone, we have a big game next week against East Valley Middle School. Everyone line up, let's get some drills started.

Beth, get over here. I'm going put you up against our new star defender."

"Beth, I noticed your game was off today, you're normally one of my best players, what's the matter?"

"Well coach, I think that Gretchen girl has been spreading rumors about me."

"Looks like you might have a bully on your hands."

"Well, what can I do?"

151

"When I think about bullying, I'm reminded of a story from one of my favorite athletes.

Would you believe that Olympic gold medalist Michael Phelps was once the victim of bullying?

Michael grew up in a small town, north of Baltimore, Maryland. At nine, his parents divorced and around the same time, Phelps was diagnosed with Attention Deficit Hyper Activity Disorder."

152

"Michael took to swimming partly because both his sisters were good swimmers, but also to find an outlet for his hyperactivity. When he started swimming he was actually afraid of putting his face under the water."

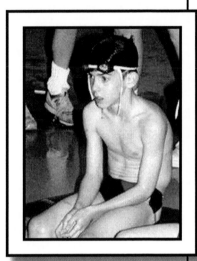

Michael was tall and gawky, with big ears and a lisp. He experienced quite a bit bullying and teasing.

"The kids used to flick my ears or throw my hat out of the school bus window."

"I got suspended when a boy flicked my ear for the hundredth time and I hit him. I was the one being bullied, yet it was me who got sent home. I can laugh about it now, but back then it really upset me. I'm well clear of it now and I thank swimming for that."

"Let's put it this way, I don't know what those kids who bullied me are doing now. They're probably still back in Baltimore. But I know one thing. They didn't go to the Beijing Olympics."

Michael Phelps – winner of 14 gold medals, the most by any Olympian. Today he is considered to be the greatest swimmer and one of the greatest Olympians of all time.

The Daily Mail Online,
May 31, 2008

"The lesson of this story is that sometimes the best way to deal with bullying is to focus on yourself. Study hard. Work hard and try to be the best you can be. Bullies will come and go but you have the rest of your life ahead of you."

"That's why I'm talking to you, Coach. Thanks for the story. I feel better."

HOMEROOM, THE NEXT AFTERNOON.

159

IN PRINCIPAL MORTON'S OFFICE

"I want to talk to you kids today about some problems I've heard you've been having with a new student."

"It's true Principal Morton, for the past few weeks the new girl, Gretchen, has been bothering us."

160

"Well kids, rest assured, we are going to get to the bottom of this.

You both should know, Gretchen isn't the only one doing the bullying. Billy and Beth, from what I've been told, you have been doing a bit of bullying as well."

"That's ridiculous!"

161

"Well let me ask you kids this, does a story about a werewolf and vampire baby ring a bell?"

"Umm...I...we were told it was a true story."

162

"The two of you are smart enough to know when a story is not true. When I spoke to Gretchen's parents about her bullying problems, they told me Gretchen was being bullied as well. They wanted me to talk to you kids about the stories you've been telling about Gretchen. Whoever participates in telling these stories is acting like a bully as well. There are lots of reasons people become bullies. One of which is that they are bullied themselves."

"Gee Mr. Morton, we never looked at it like that."

KIDS CAN BECOME BULLIES BECAUSE THEY:

- Have family problems
- Are being bullied themselves
- Are selfish or spoiled and always want to get their own way
- Have no friends and feel lonely
- Feel bad about themselves so they want to make others feel bad too
- Are taking out their own frustrations on others
- Feel **INSECURE** and unimportant - bullying gives them power
- Want to look "big" in front of others
- Have been pressured into joining a group of bullies and have gone along with things just to keep on their good side
- Don't understand how victims feel
- Get away with it, so they continue to do it

Kidscape, You Can Beat Bullying, 2005

GRETCHEN'S MEETING WITH THE SCHOOL PSYCHOLOGIST.

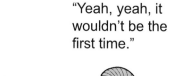

"Gretchen, a number of students, their parents, and teachers have come to me about you bullying several of your classmates. We take bullying very seriously at our school."

"Yeah, yeah, it wouldn't be the first time."

"These kids are very upset, Gretchen. You have hurt a lot of people."

"Who told on me?!? I want to know! Was it Toad or Billy Goat? I'll show them!"

ARE YOU A BULLY? PART I

- Have you ever repeatedly physically hurt someone you didn't like by kicking, punching, or shoving?

  yes ☐   **no** ☐

- Have you ever continually instructed someone else to hurt someone you disliked?

  yes ☐   **no** ☐

- Have you ever repeatedly used the Internet to hurt someone else or spread bad rumors?

  yes ☐   **no** ☐

ARE YOU A BULLY? PART II

- Have you ever tried to exclude someone from a group of friends just to hurt their feelings?

  yes ☐   **no** ☐

- Have you ever laughed or made fun of someone because of the way they look and act?

  yes ☐   **no** ☐

- Have you ever been a part of a group of kids who bullied and did nothing to stop it?

  yes ☐   **no** ☐

*If you answered **YES** to any of these questions,*

THEN THERE'S A GOOD CHANCE YOU ARE A BULLY!

WHAT IF I AM A BULLY?
HOW CAN I CHANGE?

In the adult world, it's not considered cool to hurt others. People who hurt others can end up in big trouble. They can even go to jail!

Put yourself in the shoes of the person being bullied.

How would you feel if you were the one being bullied?

"OK, so I'm a bully. So what!?! Do you have any idea what it's like to be me? Nobody likes me… I have no friends and nobody talks to me unless I make fun of people!"

"Gretchen, I'd like to tell you a story. It's a fable by Aesop called, *The Lion and the Mouse*.

There was once a mighty lion snoozing in his den. One day a foolish young mouse accidently scurried onto his back and jumped on his head.

The lion awoke angrily from his peaceful slumber. He clenched the tiny mouse in his large paws and let out a deafening roar."

"How dare you disturb my rest!?! Don't you know I am the king of the jungle!?! A small, weak creature like you should die for your actions. I should eat you right now in one quick bite."

The mouse was shaking with terror as he begged to be set free. "Please don't eat me great king. I did not mean to disturb your rest. Please, if you let me go this one time I promise to return the favor and be your friend forever. Maybe one day, I can even save your life."

"How could a puny and weak creature like you possibly save my life?" the lion chuckled. "But, little mouse, you have made me laugh and now I am in a jolly mood, so I will let you free this once."

The lion opened his mighty paw and released the mouse who quickly ran from his razor sharp claws.

"Many thanks your majesty, you will not regret this!"

Days later when the lion was out hunting, a trapper's net suddenly fell from the trees and entangled the lion. No matter how hard he tried, the lion couldn't escape. The more he struggled with his great strength, the more tangled in the net he became.

The lion let out a deafening roar heard by all the critters in the forest. Everyone was too scared to approach the lion, except the lion's new, furry little pal.

"My friend the lion is in trouble!" the mouse proclaimed, "I must go and save him at once!"

The mouse arrived to find the lion tangled in the trap.

"I will rescue you!" he declared, and with his sharp little teeth he began gnawing on the ropes.

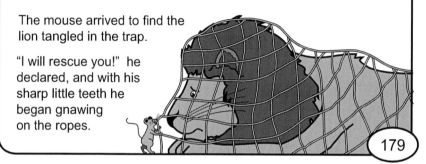

Minutes later, the lion was free.

"I was foolish to doubt you little mouse," said the lion, "I never thought you could be of any help to me, but today you have saved my life."

"I am a mouse who keeps my promises." the mouse said proudly. "I promised to return the favor and now I have."

181

182

HOW GRETCHEN CAN CHANGE:

- Treat others how she wants to be treated

- Be accepting of all people

- Choose her words carefully

- Be considerate of others' space

- Respect others' property

If you bully other kids to make yourself feel better and want to put a stop to your behavior remember *The Golden Rule*: talk to an adult.

Don't be afraid of getting in trouble, you are doing the right thing and should be proud of yourself for taking action.

BACK IN PRINCIPAL MORTON'S OFFICE WITH BILLY AND BETH

"Billy and Beth, we look to you as leaders in the sixth grade. That is why Gretchen's parents wanted me to tell you that deep down inside, Gretchen wants to be your friend. Did you know *The Wizard of Oz* is her favorite movie? She was very sad that she didn't get a chance to audition for the play."

LATER, ON THE PLAYGROUND.

189

190

191

BILLY, BETH, AND GRETCHEN TALK FOR HOURS. IT TURNS OUT THAT THEY HAVE A LOT IN COMMON... FROM SOCCER TO MUSIC TO VIDEO GAMES.

"My parents just got me the new Wii Fit."

"Awesome! Can we come play with you sometime?"

192

Billy and Beth didn't realize was that by participating in the spreading of the rumors about Gretchen being a monster, they were indirectly bullying her as well.

Sometimes kids might not realize they are engaged in bullying. Take some time to reflect on how you treat others. Even kids who are bullied can be bullies themselves.

"When I saw you in those costumes, I was so jealous. *The Wizard of Oz* is my favorite movie. I heard auditions for the play were over by the time I got to Stickville, and I guess I bullied you to make myself feel better."

"You know Gretchen, they're still looking for someone to play the part of the wicked witch. We can talk to Mr. French, the director, and maybe get you the part."

THE NEXT DAY AT PLAY REHEARSAL

Gretchen, Billy, Beth, Ronnie, and Lester became friends practicing very hard for the 6th grade play.

They are looking forward to finally being able to perform on stage together.

STICKVILLE MIDDLE SCHOOL'S 6TH GRADE PROUDLY PRESENTS A VERY SPECIAL PERFORMANCE OF:

205

206

207

"Courage! What makes the sphinx the seventh wonder? Courage! What makes the dawn come up like thunder? Courage! What makes the Hottentot so hot? What puts the "ape" in apricot? What have they got that I ain't got?" - *The Wizard of Oz*

208

209

AFTER THE PLAY

"Hey you little creep. Do you actually think you're a dog or something? Well a dog doesn't need his lunch money!"

"Watch it right there Logan!"

210

211

212

213

Well, that concludes our story!
"GOODBYE"
from all of us and
thanks for reading!

214

CONCLUSION

I hope you enjoyed my story. It looks like everything worked out for the Stickville Middle School 6th graders. I want to make an important point, however, that not all tales end in friendship like this one. The most important idea presented in this book is to put a <u>stop</u> to bullying in any shape or form. If you use the strategies presented in this book you can develop a gameplan to effectively put an end to bullying.

To learn more about bullying and receive future updates. Check out our website: **http://theskinnyon.com/bullyingblog**

Email us: **bullying@theskinnyon.com**

GLOSSARY

Golden Rule: Always talk to an adult when you experience bullying of any kind. This person can be a teacher, parent, coach or any adult you trust.

Bystander: Someone who observes bullying, but does nothing to stop it.

Bullying: Happens when someone hurts or scares another person on purpose and the person being bullied has a hard time defending him or herself. Usually, bullying happens over and over.

Bullying Policy: In your school this would be a set of rules and procedures for what behavior is unacceptable and what actions will be taken if bullying or cyberbullying take place.

Target: Someone who is easily bullied and has a hard time defending him or herself.

Henchmen: People who support a bully either by encouraging the bully or actively engaging in the bullying activity.

Ally: Somebody who is on your side and willing to support you.

Hot Spots: Unsupervised areas where bullies tend to hang out and pick on people.

Verbal Bullying: Using words to hurt others.

Physical Bullying: Intentionally hurting someone with force.

Indirect Bullying: When you hurt someone behind their back, not to their face.

Cyberbullying: Bullying that happens online or electronically. When children or teens bully each other using the Internet, mobile phones, or other forms of technology.

Posing: Pretending to be somebody else online often to behave in ways that offend others or humiliate the person who is being impersonated.

Flaming: Fights between two people in text or e-mail messages.

Insecure: Subject to fears and doubts. Lacking self-confidence.

BIBLIOGRAPHY/ RESOURCE PAGE

US Department of Health and Human Services (Stop Bullying Now!):
http://www.stopbullyingnow.hrsa.gov/kids/

National Crime Prevention Council:
http://www.ncpc.org/

Cyberbullying:
http://www.ncpc.org/cyberbullying

Publications and resources for educators, parents, and community members. From the California Department of Education:
http://www.cde.ca.gov/ls/ss/se/bullyres.asp

This section of girlshealth.gov gives the low-down on bullying among girls, which is more common than you might think:
http://www.girlshealth.gov/bullying/

FindYouthInfo.gov was created by the Interagency Working Group on Youth Programs (IWGYP), which is composed of representatives from 12 Federal agencies that support programs and services focusing on youth:
http://www.findyouthinfo.org/topic_bullying.shtml

Government of Alberta Children and Youth Services. Bullying resources and celebrity testimonials:
http://www.b-free.ca

Further reading and parent guides:
http://theskinnyon.com/bullyingblog

Pssst ... get
the skinny on™
life's most
important lessons

Join **The Skinny On**™
community today!

- Get 20% off your first
  purchase

- Receive exclusive offers,
  previews and discounts

- See excerpts from all
  The Skinny On™ books

- Suggest topics for
  new books

- View and subscribe to
  The Skinny On™
  weekly webcomic

- Become a writer for
  The Skinny On™

www.TheSkinnyOn.com

Connect with us on: